REAL ESTATE TIPS

FOR THE SAVVY HOME BUYER AND SELLER

GILLIAN CUNNINGHAM

Limits of Liability / Disclaimer of Warranty:
Tips in this book are for informational purposes only. The publisher and author have used their best efforts in preparing this book. They make no representations or warranties with respect to the accuracy or completeness of the contents of this book and specifically disclaim any implied warranties or fitness for a particular purpose.

No warranty may be created or extended by sales representatives or consumers. Neither the publisher nor author shall be liable for any loss of profit or any other damages, including but not limited to special, incidental or consequential damages.

Ordering information:
Quantity sales. Special discounts are available on quantity purchases by corporations, associations, and others. For details, contact the author at the address above. Orders by U.S. trade bookstores and wholesalers.

Printed in United States of America.

DEDICATION

This book is dedicated to you, the prospective home buyer and seller, to help maximize your time and money and put you one step ahead in the real estate process.

FOREWORD

I am deeply honored to write the foreword for this book.

In 2005, Gillian and I were speakers at a Real Estate Marketing Roundtable. In the first five minutes of her presentation, Gillian gave voice to one of my long-held beliefs: "Real estate is a wealth creation tool. As a real estate agent, you are encouraged to become an investor so that you can teach your clients how to do the same."

As Gillian gave voice to this, questions started swirling around the success mindset used to build her then firm "Prestique Realty," as well as the best practices for educating buyers and sellers. Gillian proceeded to pass out a handout called "The Ten 'Buyer' Commandments." The purpose of it was to remind buyers of the pitfalls that can derail a transaction from closing. After the meeting, I jokingly said that those tips would make a great mini book for fellow agents and brokers. Gillian chuckled and said, "Kadena, thank you. My schedule is really hectic right now serving clients." Imagine my delight that you are reading this book almost 14 years later.

Gillian Cunningham is a phenomenal Real Estate Broker and advocate for the empowerment of real estate consumers. Gillian believes in abundance and the power of sharing information.

This book is for home buyers, sellers, and agents, who, like Gillian, desire to be proactive in their real estate transactions. As a result of reading and applying the tips highlighted in this book, you will have a keen sense of what to expect during the real estate process and be better prepared to navigate a transaction with confidence.

Kadena Tate

Author. Speaker. Thought Provoker. Revenue Strategist.

www.KadenaTate.com

TABLE OF CONTENTS

INTRODUCTION

For years, I have offered tips to my clients to prepare them for their home buying or home selling experience. Many of them have commented on how useful the tips were. So, I thought if my clients found the tips useful, other consumers may as well, hence, *Real Estate Tips for the Savvy Home Buyer & Seller*.

I hope you find a few pearls you can apply to help you navigate the real estate process and that your overall experience is all the better for it.

HINT: *You'll find bolded terms throughout the book. If a term is unfamiliar to you, check the glossary for a definition.*

PART ONE

FOR BUYERS

BUYER PREPARATION TIPS

BUYER PREPARATION TIPS

WHY HIRE A BUYER'S AGENT?

Hire a **Buyer's Agent** to benefit from their knowledge, experience, and expertise. The Buyer Agent represents you and can give you advice and guidance.

A **Buyer's Agent** looks out for your best interest and assists you with your property search, pricing, terms, contracts, negotiations, etc.

Hire a full-time agent who will solely focus on the purchase of your new home, not a part-time one who has other things vying for their time and attention.

Buying new construction?
Hire a Buyer Agent. Remember,
the SALESPERSON represents
the Builder and LOOKS OUT
FOR THE BUILDER'S BEST
INTEREST, not yours.

When nothing else but "new" will do—NEW CONSTRUCTION, that is—HIRE A BUYER'S AGENT to get the best deal.

BUYER PREPARATION TIPS

FINANCING

Did you know you can buy a home for as little as 3.5-5% down? Yes, you can!

20% **down payment** isn't a requirement to purchase a home. 52% of **buyers** put down less.

Thinking about buying a home but not sure if you qualify? Yes, you can pull up an online calculator, but your best bet is to contact a lender to see if you qualify and what's needed to be ready when the time is right.

Have a **mortgage lender** pull your **credit** 3-6 months in advance so there are no surprises with your credit.

Figure out how much you can afford. Better yet, decide how much you're willing to pay. Remember, just because you qualify for a larger **mortgage** doesn't mean you want to have that kind of payment each month.

Get pre-approved for **financing** so you'll know how much you qualify for and to strengthen your negotiating power.

No money down does not mean no money needed. You still need **earnest money**, **option fees**, inspection fees, and possible **closing costs**.

Closing costs typically range between 3-6% of the **purchase price**.

Thinking of buying a home? Open a savings account just for your **down payment**, and then make automatic monthly contributions.

Buying a house in a year or two?
Save money. CASH IS KING!

Buying a property with cash or **financing** with few to no **seller requests** and a fast **closing** is often appealing to sellers.

CASH BUYER? That's great!
Be prepared to provide proof of
funds in the form of a financial or
bank statement.

Financing your purchase? Large banking institutions aren't necessarily better. Consult with a local mortgage company to compare.

What's the difference between 4% and 5% **interest rates**?*

Most people think it's 1%. The real question is... How does this 1% affect your monthly payment? On $300,000, 1% could add $180/mo. On $400,000, 1% could add $235/mo.

Consult a lender for interest rate impact.

Do not use credit cards excessively. Doing so could affect your loan **debt-to-income ratio** and ultimately your ability to qualify for a **mortgage**.

BUYER DO'S & DON'TS

For the most accurate property status and information, visit www.Realtor.com.

Do you have a list of must-haves in your new home? Remember, some features can be changed after you purchase.

Because you may change jobs, don't make close proximity to your current employer a primary factor when making your decision. Consider other factors like neighborhood or area **amenities**.

Are you a pet lover or owner of an aggressive breed or exotic pet? Before buying a home, check city laws or **HOA** guidelines to make sure there are no pet restrictions.

When buying a property, think RESALE VALUE. Location and condition will be key factors.

Write down the addresses of properties of interest and then forward them to your Buyer's Agent to research.

Do not call the number on a yard sign or email an agent on the internet to inquire about a property. Let your Buyer's Agent do so. Otherwise, you could compromise your negotiations.

New construction homes typically come with a **builder's warranty**. Check to see what's covered.

Contact your lender to determine
the **financing**
best for you.

Earnest money can vary depending on the price of the property. In a Seller's Market, 1% of the sales price is customary, but in some cases, it can be significantly lower.

Familiarize yourself with the **termination option**, which allows the buyer to conduct inspections with the unrestricted right to terminate the contract.

BUYER SHOWING TIPS

When viewing a property with
your agent, come prepared
to purchase.

Photos can be deceiving. If a property meets your criteria, view it in person before you dismiss it.

Know that there is no perfect home, even if you build it from the ground up. There's always something that you may desire to change.

When you view properties, rate them on a scale of 1 to 10 with 10 being perfect and 5 being average. Since it's hard to find a "perfect" home, properties rated 7 or 8 should be given serious "**offer**" consideration.

After viewing multiple properties,
rank them 1st, 2nd, or 3rd based
on whether you can see yourself
living in
the house.

Pay attention to **curb appeal** and floor plan functionality. Keep in mind, some things cannot be changed, but cosmetic things like wall colors, light fixtures, faucets, and flooring can.

If you see a house you like but the kitchen backsplash and countertops are not to your liking, know that you can change them out for a relatively nominal cost.

A home buying checklist can help you keep track of what you need and what you want in a home. A need is a feature that is essential in your home and a want is a desired feature that is not mandatory.

In-law suites are a smart feature, gaining in popularity. Some are used to accommodate family but may be used for a small business or long-term rental.

When looking at properties, visualize yourself living in the home. If you can imagine your family and furniture in the home, you may want to give serious consideration to submitting an **offer**.

Keep in mind, you're not just buying a house; you're buying a community.

When house hunting, consider access to **amenities**, which may make life enjoyable in your community.

If you love a property, make an **offer**. The worst thing you can do is wait. The house may not be available when you
come back.

In a **seller's market**, if competing against multiple **offers**, KEEP OFFERS CLEAN. Secure the contract and then negotiate additional items during the **option period**.

When buying new construction,
plan to live in the property at
least 3-5 years unless the
community is in closeout.
Otherwise, you'll be competing
against the builder
when you sell.

BUYER CONTRACT-TO-CLOSE TIPS

BUYER CONTRACT-TO-CLOSE TIPS

INSPECTIONS

There are two types of inspections:

1) Mechanical

2) Wood-Destroying Insect

Always, *always* get a **mechanical inspection**, whether you're purchasing a new home or an existing one. This way you receive an unbiased third-party report
on the condition of
the property.

Mechanical inspections evaluate the roof, foundation, heating, cooling, electrical, and plumbing components, as well as appliances, windows, doors, etc.

When inspecting an existing property, your main concerns should be whether or not there are any major mechanical issues with the roof, foundation, heating, cooling, plumbing, and electrical components. If issues exist, address them with the **seller**.

Wood destroying insect (WDI) inspections determine the presence or absence of termites, carpenter ants, wood-boring beetles, etc.

WDI inspections can be optional when purchasing new construction properties since the wood is new and, in most cases, has been treated. However, with existing properties, it is highly recommended that you get one.

Inspections are not just to identify issues. They can also provide estimates on the lifespan of various components in the home.

Show up for the last 30 minutes of the inspection for an overview and to see any issues firsthand. This will serve as a point of reference when reviewing the inspection report later.

BUYER CONTRACT-TO-CLOSE TIPS

BEFORE CLOSING

Do not buy furniture, appliances, or other household items until after you close. Doing so may increase your **debt-to-income ratio** and compromise your loan approval.

Do not change jobs, quit your job, give notice to quit, or become self-employed right before **closing**. Doing so may cause lenders to question your ability to pay your **mortgage** and result in loan denial.

Do not buy a car, truck, or van while under contract. Again, doing so may increase your **debt-to-income ratio** and compromise your loan approval.

Do not make large deposits into your bank account without checking with your loan officer. All funds must be accounted for. Gift funds can only come from parents.

Do not co-sign purchases, credit cards, or loans for anyone. Additional debt will increase your **debt-to-income ratio** and could compromise your loan approval.

Do not spend money you've set aside for the **down payment** or **closing costs**. Vacations and shopping can wait, but your contractual obligations to purchase a property may not.

Bring your **repair amendment** to your final walkthrough to make sure repairs are completed.

BUYER CONTRACT-TO-CLOSE TIPS

AFTER CLOSING

Contact a locksmith to re-key the locks in your new home.

Even if you don't have a **mortgage**, it is wise to keep homeowner's insurance to cover your personal property and unforeseen circumstances, such as natural disasters or accidents on your property.

There's more to owning a home than the **mortgage** payment. Be prepared for other expenses:

1. Property Taxes
2. Insurance
3. Lawn care
4. Unexpected repairs

BUYER
MOVING TIPS

Don't forget to let the post office know you're moving in advance. You can fill out the form online and give the exact date you want your mail
to be forwarded!

Do your research on moving companies. Some companies provide free onsite estimates and even provide boxes for packing.

Get estimates or quotes from moving companies and create a moving budget.

Order your supplies! Make sure to order boxes, tape, bubble wrap, and permanent markers to arrive before your moving day so you can start packing as soon as possible.

Start using your perishable items that you don't want to have to move.

Purge, purge, purge!
If you haven't used or worn an
item in two years or more,
consider donating it to charity.
You may be able to receive a
tax deduction.

Label your moving boxes, and then make a list of what is in each box to stay organized and make unpacking easier!

Transfer your kids' school records
to their new school so everyone
is ready when
school starts.

Give the moving company driver directions to your new home.

Before moving in and unpacking, check to see if you need to repaint. This can alleviate the need to move things twice.

PART TWO

FOR
SELLERS

SELLER PREPARATION TIPS

Hire a Realtor to sell your home. Realtors can assist with a marketing plan, property preparation, property exposure, contracts, negotiations, and more.

INTERIOR PREPARATION

Remember, how you live in your house is not how you sell your house.

Staging can increase your bottom line.

Hire a property stager. Furniture and accessory placement can make or break a sale.

Make your house "show ready!"
Declutter, depersonalize
and neutralize.

Declutter—pack away items that you are not using (seasonal clothing, small appliances, refrigerator magnets, collectibles, etc.). This will make your home look cleaner and larger.

Depersonalize—remove all personal photos, unique art, etc. This way the buyer doesn't come into the house looking at your photos and art trying to figure out who currently lives in the house instead of visualizing themselves living there.

Neutralize—if your rooms are different colors, paint a soft cream, yellow, beige, or gray.

When preparing your property to sell, choose natural palettes—warm grays, taupe, or rich browns.

Remove outdated wallpaper. Most people are visual. If buyers envision a need to make a change to the property, this sometimes will come at a cost to the seller. So, make the property move-in ready.

If you're a hunter and collect animal heads or stuffed fish, unless you live in the country or a rural area, it's recommended that you remove them so as not to offend or frighten the buyer.

If you have more than three flooring types (tile, carpet, wood, etc.) that can be seen from any one room in the house, you may consider changing them.

Consider upgrading your appliances. Buyers put premiums on upgraded, high-quality appliances.

Dirty entry or kitchen floor tile
grout can be a turnoff
to buyers.

Hire a cleaning service for a thorough top-to-bottom scrubbing.

Professionally clean the carpets. You'd be amazed at what a clean carpet does.

Replace worn carpet or rugs.

New updated light fixtures can add monetary value to your sales price.

A functional decorative ceiling fan is a beautiful thing.

Bathroom updates are always a smart investment.

Freshen up your bathrooms by changing the faucets and light fixtures.

Re-caulk the shower and
tub surround.

Remove popcorn ceilings.
Popcorn is for the movies.

Clean the windows.
Clean windows make the
home look brighter.

Let the sunshine in. Open blinds or drapes and turn on lights.

SMART hands-free technology is becoming very popular. Voice command or digitally managed equipment may add value to the sale of your home.

Keep up with regular
maintenance and repairs.

Selling your house in the spring? Add light, bright-colored accent pillows to your sofa or change bedroom comforters to make the room come alive.

Selling your house in the fall? Sprinkle in a little autumn—deep reds, oranges, and golden yellow—in table décor, towels, accent rugs, and even artwork.

Houses sell year-round no matter the season. Fall and winter offer less seller competition because there
are fewer properties on the market. So, take advantage! Buyers are waiting.

EXTERIOR PREPARATION

Think **curb appeal**. How does your home look when the buyer drives up? If you only have greenery or shrubs out front, add a pop of color. Plant a flat of flowers at the front door or purchase a colorful potted plant.

Add a fresh layer of mulch to your flowerbeds.

To freshen up the exterior of your property, consider pressure washing or repaving your driveway.

Change old, rusted light fixtures.

Trim your trees and clean your gutters.

Add shelving to increase storage space in a closet or the garage. This can add value to the sale of your house.

Service the air conditioner and heating system.

Be proactive. Get a **pre-listing inspection** so you know what's going on with your property before the buyer finds out.

A **pre-listing inspection** enables you to repair identified issues, get estimates on how much it will cost to repair them, or price your property accordingly based on the repairs needed.

SELLER SHOWING TIPS

SELLER SHOWING TIPS

SELLER DO'S & DON'TS

Think **curb appeal**. A buyer's first impression is determined by your property's curb appeal.

Manicure the lawn. Keep it mowed and edged. Reseed or sod bare spots.

Boost your **curb appeal** by
painting or staining
the front door.

Create a welcoming entrance.
Purchase a door mat.

"Professional photography"—not cell phone photography—can make a big difference when selling a property.

Open your blinds or drapes for property **showings**. Dark homes look smaller to buyers and sometimes feel like caves. Brighter homes are more appealing.

Before **showing** your home, put away valuables and prescriptions and secure all firearms.

Consider leaving your Smart Home equipment as a home purchase incentive.

Add fresh flowers to make a
room come alive and feel
more inviting.

Your backyard is an extension of your house. Manicure the lawn and remove tattered furniture.

Make a property highlights sheet to emphasize updates or recent repairs.

Do not turn down or cancel a **showing**. Doing so could increase the time your property spends on the market and ultimately attract lower **offers**.

SELLER CONTRACT-TO-CLOSE TIPS

Property disclosure: if you intentionally withhold information, you are committing fraud.

During a buyer's home inspection, make sure the inspector has access to all areas of the property (crawlspaces, attics, service panels, water heaters, etc.).

After a buyer's inspection, repair requests are often made.

Be open to repairs requested by buyers. Provide receipts and details of recent repairs.

Repairs are negotiable. However, if you choose to address repairs, consider offering a repair credit to allow the buyer to handle repairs themselves.

Never send personal information via email (bank accounts, social security numbers, etc.). Call your agent or title company if that information is requested.

Planning to leave your refrigerator? Don't mention it in your marketing. Use it as a point of negotiation if repairs are needed.

SELLER MOVING TIPS

Clean the house before move-out. Think of how you would like to receive your new home if you were buying.

Leave instructions for the buyers on how to operate appliances or technology
left behind.

Create a list of local service providers to make the buyer's moving transition a little smoother.

CLOSING REMARKS

I hope you found these tips helpful and you feel a little more confident in navigating the real estate process.

Remember these three things: 1) whether you are buying or selling a property, hire a real estate agent to represent you and your property; 2) inspections are important for both buyers and sellers; and 3) real estate can be a wealth creation tool.

If you have a friend or family member looking to buy or sell a property, pay it forward... buy a copy for them.

— Gillian Cunningham

GLOSSARY

Amenities

> Features that enhance the property but are not essential to the property's use. Examples include, but are not limited to, swimming pools, fitness centers, tennis courts, playgrounds, gardens, or beach access.

> October 2019. *Selling Guide Glossary*. Retrieved from https://www.fanniemae.com/content/guide/selling/e/3/glossary.html

Builder's warranty

> Provided by the builder on new construction properties and typically covers defects on workmanship, materials, structural components, foundation and appliances for a specified period of time after the purchase.

Buyer

> Individual or business entity that purchases a property.

Buyer's Agent

Real Estate Agent or Broker who represents the buyer in a transaction. One who looks out for the best interest of the buyer. Services are typically free to the buyer because the seller, in their listing agreement, has agreed to pay the fees of the seller's agent and the buyer's agent.

January 2019. *What is Buyer's Agent?* Retrieved from https://www.redfin.com/definition/buyers-agent

Buyer's market

Occurs when the supply (available homes for sale) exceeds demand (the number of buyers seeking to purchase homes).

January 2019. *What is a Buyer's vs. Seller's Market?* Retrieved from https://www.redfin.com/guides/buyers-market-vs-sellers-market

Closing (date)

Also referred to as settlement, the final step in executing a real estate transaction; the phase when ownership of the property is transferred to the buyer and the transaction is completed.

August 2019. *Closing (Real Estate).* Retrieved from https://en.wikipedia.org/wiki/Closing_(real_estate)

Closing costs

Fees paid at closing by the buyer or seller. Typically includes but not limited to loan origination fee, title examination and insurance, survey, attorney's fee, and prepaid items, such as escrow deposits for taxes and insurance.

October 2019. *Selling Guide Glossary*. Retrieved from https://www.fanniemae.com/content/guide/selling/e/3/glossary.html

Credit score

A statistical number that evaluates a person's creditworthiness based on credit history. Credit scores range from 300 to 850. The higher the score, the more financially trustworthy a person is considered to be.

Kagan, Julia (2019). *Credit Sore*. Retrieved from https://www.investopedia.com/terms/c/credit_score.asp

Curb appeal

The visual attractiveness of a house as seen from the street.

Merriam-Webster Dictionary. Curb Appeal. 2019. *Curb Appeal*. Retrieved from https://www.merriam-webster.com/dictionary/curb%20appeal

Debt-to-income ratio

A ratio derived by dividing the borrower's total monthly obligations (including housing expense) by the borrower's monthly income. This calculation is used to determine the mortgage amount for which a borrower qualifies.

October 2019. *Selling Guide Glossary.* Retrieved from https://www.fanniemae.com/content/guide/selling/e/3/glossary.html

Down payment

The amount of money a buyer pays at closing to fund a home purchase, usually expressed as a percentage of the total home price.

January 2019. *What is down payment in Real Estate?* Retrieved from https://www.redfin.com/definition/down-payment

Earnest money

Money submitted with a purchase offer to show the buyer's offer is being made in good faith.

Financing

The act of obtaining money to purchase a property.

Dictionary.com. Financing. 2019. *Financing*. Retrieved from https://www.dictionary.com/browse/financing

HOA (Homeowners' Association)

An organization in a subdivision, planned community or condominium that makes and enforces rules for the properties and their residents. Those who purchase property within an HOA's jurisdiction automatically become members and are required to pay dues, known as HOA dues. Some associations can be very restrictive about what members can do with their properties.

Chen, James (2019). *Homeowners Association - HOA*. Retrieved from www.investopedia.com/terms/h/hoa.asp

Interest rate

The amount a lender charges for the use of assets expressed as a percentage of the principal. The interest rate is typically noted on an annual basis known as the Annual Percentage Rate (APR).

Banton, Caroline (2019). *Interest Rate*. Retrieved from https://www.investopedia.com/terms/i/interestrate.asp

Mechanical inspection

A detailed examination of the major components of a property with a focus on, but not limited to, the roof, foundation, heating, cooling, electrical and plumbing systems.

Mortgage (loan)

Funds borrowed from a mortgage lender to finance the purchase of a home. Conventional loans, FHA loans and VA loans are a few different types of mortgage loans available.

January 2019. *What is a mortgage loan?* Retrieved from https://www.redfin.com/definition/mortgage-loan

Mortgage Lender

A person or company that loans money and takes a security interest in real property.

The Complete Real Estate Encyclopedia by Denise L. Evans, JD & O. William Evans, JD. 2007 "Mortgage Lender". Retrieved from https://financial-dictionary.thefreedictionary.com/mortgage+lender

Offer

A conditional proposal made by a buyer or seller to buy or sell a property, which becomes legally enforceable if accepted.

Kenton, Will (2018). *What is an Offer.* Retrieved from https://www.investopedia.com/terms/o/offer.asp

Option fee and period

In Texas, the negotiated fee buyers pay sellers to have the unrestricted right to terminate the contract during a certain timeframe, typically 1-10 days. If buyers terminate contract during this time, the buyers only forfeit their option fee but not their earnest money.

Pre-listing inspection

A property examination by an unbiased 3rd Party Inspector conducted before a seller puts their property on the market to determine if there are any issues with the property. Upon completion, sellers can choose to either repair items before buyers find out, obtain repair estimates to negotiate if buyers would like issue repaired or price property accordingly without repairs.

Property disclosure

A disclosure from the seller making the buyer aware of the seller's knowledge of the condition of the property.

Purchase price

The price a buyer pays for a property.

Repair amendment

A request created by the buyer during the option period to have repairs to completed by the seller. Repairs are negotiable. The seller may agree to all repairs, agree to some repairs or not agree to any repairs.

Seller

The individual or business entity that sells a property.

Seller requests

When a buyer asks the seller for negotiable items in the buyer's offer.

Seller's/Owner's Agent

A real estate agent or broker who represents the owner of a property for sale.

Seller's market

Occurs when demand exceeds supply, or there are more buyers seeking to purchase homes than there are available homes on the market. This often leads to multiple buyers interested in a single property, resulting in bidding wars.

January 2019. *What is a Buyer's Market vs. Seller's Market?* Retrieved from www.redfin.com/guides/buyers-market-vs-sellers-market

Showing

A property viewing by a buyer.

Staging

The act of preparing a private residence for sale in the real estate marketplace. The goal of staging is to make a home appealing to the highest number of potential buyers, thereby selling a property more swiftly and for more money.

November 2019. *Home Staging.* Retrieved from https://en.wikipedia.org/wiki/Home_staging

Termination option

> A clause that allows real estate buyers to back out of a purchase contract during a fixed period of time that precedes its official closing date. It is useful for buyers who wish to take a closer look at the terms of the purchase contract and the state of the parcel that they wish to purchase.
>
> November 2013. *What is the Termination Option?* Retrieved from https://info.courthousedirect.com/blog/bid/340933/what-is-the-termination-option

WDI inspection

> A property inspection to determine the presence and accessibility of wood destroying insects.

ABOUT THE AUTHOR

Gillian Cunningham's name is synonymous with true professionalism, extraordinary knowledge, exceptional customer service, strong work ethic, and high integrity standards. Gillian's personal approach and no-nonsense negotiating skills have landed her as an invaluable asset to her real estate clients.

A graduate from the University of Kansas with degrees in Mechanical Engineering and Business Administration, Gillian worked in corporate America for IBM and Phillips Petroleum prior to obtaining her Real Estate license and Broker's license in 2002 and 2005, respectively. Gillian's eagerness to stay on top of her industry led her to earn designations as Certified Residential Specialist, Accredited Buyer Representative, and Accredited Staging Professional.

An avid business-to-business networker, Gillian has been featured in *Texas Monthly* magazine, *Natural Awakenings* magazine, and *Community Impact* newspaper. In 2013 and for 7 consecutive years through the printing of this book, Gillian was also recognized as a Five Star Real Estate Professional—representing less than two percent of Realtors® in the North Texas area.

Gillian's personal goal is to empower clients to make informed real estate decisions and to grow her community one satisfied family at a time.

Got a real estate question or need assistance with your next real estate transaction? Gillian is a Broker Associate with eXp Realty serving the Greater Dallas/Fort Worth Texas metroplex. Contact Gillian at:

Ask@GillianCunningham.com

Or visit: www.GillianCunningham.com.

Connect with Gillian on Social Media using **AskGillianCunningham** on Instagram, Facebook and LinkedIn or **AskGillian** on "X" (formerly known asTwitter).

As Gillian always says,

"Make your NEXT MOVE your BEST MOVE!"

ACKNOWLEDGMENTS

I would like to recognize my mother for being my first true love, for always encouraging me to be all that I could be, for expanding my view of the world beyond my neighborhood and for allowing me to dream.

To my dear friends, male and female, you know who you are, for your gentle nudges to keep moving forward.

And to my clients, who reaffirmed my tips and suggestions had value. I heard each of you. Thank you.